MONSTER KNOWS
MORE THAN,
LESS THAN

BY LORI CAPOTE   ILLUSTRATED BY CHIP WASS

PICTURE WINDOW BOOKS
a capstone imprint

We're all at
MONSTER FAIR,
comparing numbers for fun!

We'll use **MORE THAN** >

and **LESS THAN.** <

CAN YOU HELP US GET THE JOB DONE?

Which is the **CREEPIER** monster?
Look at the snakes in their hair!

The red one has **7 SNAKES** hissing.
Is that **MORE THAN** the blue
monster's share?

7 > 5

This slimy ride spins round and round.
Who has **MORE EYES** that twirl?

He has **4**,
and that's much **MORE** than
the 1-eyed monster girl.

4 > 1

Which **BENCH** is better for resting?

8

They both have these
flowers that **STINK.**

Let's sit here. It has **FEWER** roses.
EEEW—they are **SMELLY** and **PINK!**

4 < 7

Where should I sit for lunch?

By the monster with **MORE** food to share!

YUM! It's snails on a stick!

She has **MORE**,
so I'm sitting right there.

6 > 5

Which coaster should I ride?

The one that has **FEWER** drops.

The Snake has **3** GIANT HILLS!
The Bunny has **FEWER**—then stops.

2 < 3

Which flavor ice cream do you like?
Mint-bug or
worm-berry goop?

The cone that's my **FAVORITE** treat?

Of course, it's the one with **MORE** scoops!

5 > 3

How many balloons can
I pop at this game?
I want some AWESOME, GROSS PRIZES!

First I pop **7**, and then I bust **LESS**.

Rotten apples are **LOVELY SURPRISES!**

17

I'm low on my carnival cash.

I must spend **LESS** money to ride.

HOW MUCH does it cost for the fun house?

1 < 2

Is it **LESS THAN** the cool cactus slide?

Which bumper car should I choose?

MORE TIRES on one car are flat.

4 > 3

Flat tires make the ride so bumpy.

I LI-LI-LI-LIKE THAT!

All day we found things at the fair
we could **COUNT**,
so we didn't just **GUESS**.

By comparing all
of the numbers,
we had a great day,
MORE OR LESS!

Internet Sites

FactHound offers a safe, fun way to find Internet sites related to this book. All of the sites on FactHound have been researched by our staff.

Here's all you do:

Visit *www.facthound.com*

Type in this code: 9781404879478

Super-cool stuff!

Check out projects, games and lots more at **www.capstonekids.com**

Look for all the books in the series:

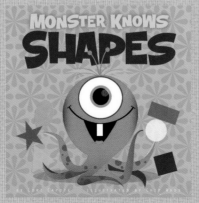

Thanks to our adviser for his expertise, research, and advice:
Terry Flaherty, PhD, Professor of English
Minnesota State University, Mankato

Editor: Shelly Lyons
Designer: Ashlee Suker
Art Director: Nathan Gassman
Production Specialist: Laura Manthe
The illustrations in this book were created digitally.

Picture Window Books are published by Capstone,
1710 Roe Crest Drive, North Mankato, Minnesota 56003
www.capstonepub.com

Library of Congress Cataloging-in-Publication Data
Capote, Lori, 1966-
Monster knows more than, less than / by Lori Capote ;
illustrated by Chip Wass.
pages cm. — (Monster knows math)
ISBN 978-1-4048-7947-8 (library binding)
ISBN 978-1-4048-8039-9 (board book)
ISBN 978-1-4795-0182-3 (ebook PDF)
1. Number concept—Juvenile literature. I. Wass, Chip, 1965-
illustrator. II. Title.
QA141.15.C365 2013
512.7—dc23   2012029715

Artistic Effects
Shutterstock, background texture (throughout)

Printed in the United States of America in
North Mankato, Minnesota.
092012   006933CGS13